Fruit-Infused Water Recipes

Recipes for your water bottle infuser, pitcher or jar

14 Peaks

DISCLAIMER

All articles, information, and resources published in this eBook are based on the individual author's opinions and are meant only to motivate readers to make their own nutrition and health decisions after consulting with their health care provider.

Authors are not and do not wish to portray to be doctors or medical professionals. All readers should consult a doctor before making any health changes, especially any changes related to a specific diagnosis or condition. All information contained in this eBook is the sole opinion of the author and contributors.

Any statements or claims about the possible health benefits conferred by any foods or supplements within this eBook have not been evaluated by the Food and Drug Administration and are not intended to diagnose, treat, cure, or prevent any disease.

Table of Contents

Introduction

Welcome to the wonderful world of fruit-infused water, where you get all the big benefits of water and a splash of fresh and fabulous fruity flavor to go along with it. Read on to find out why this book is making waves!

You just can't get any better than water when it comes to drinking in great health. Or can you? Learn how fruit water recipes combine fruit and water together to synergistically bring you the ultimate beverages for your health and your taste buds too.

Not only will you find out how water helps your body to function, you'll learn how all water is not created equally. You'll get helpful hints in distinguishing the good from the bad so you can start your water infusion recipes out right.

Fruit brings bursts of nutrients and health benefits to the table, or to the bottle in this case. You are about to find out hidden secrets that lay beyond the peel and skin of some of the most scrumptious fruits on the planet.

Did you know that blueberries are one of the most potent anti-oxidant fruits in existence? They are great for your immune system, excellent for your heart and awesome for your skin. Did you know that cucumbers are loaded with vitamins and also keep your body temperature balanced and your body hydrated? Did you know that a cucumber is not a vegetable? It's a fruit.

Explore additional ingredients that can complement your flavored water recipes and what medicinal values they hold. For instance, peppermint adds a minty fresh twist of flavor and pain-relieving qualities as well. Ginger is an anti-inflammatory that also calms queasy stomachs.

Although this book is swimming with important and interesting information about both water and fruit, the finale is the delicious, tantalizing fruit-infused water recipes. You will receive step-by-step instructions and a summary of the health benefits from each creative concoction that is both delicious and intriguing.

Find basic beginner fruit water recipes as well as delicious detox drink recipes, flavored water recipes for weight-loss and the best recipes for drinks that will pull your body back together after a strenuous workout. You'll also get healing water-infused recipes for a myriad of medical issues.

To top the book off, you will find tons of tips that will save you time and money when it comes to making your flavored water recipes.

Don't waste another minute. Let's dive in now…shall we?

Chapter 1
Get a Splash out of Fruits

Fruits are a splash! They are so delicious you just want to drink them down to the last drop. Fruit infusions let you do exactly that. Convenient, portable and healthy, you are about to learn how to infuse fruits for the ultimate refreshing drink ever.

Health Benefits

Did you know that if you infuse fruits into your water as a regular part of your daily diet, scientists say you will be less prone to chronic diseases? Not only that, you'll even ward away more common ailments like migraines, digestive issues and even fatigue. There are practically no calories, cholesterol, sodium and fats in fruit-infused water and absolutely no side effects. It's a win-win all the way around!

First Things First

Whether you are a novice or expert in the fruit infusion world, you will need to begin it all with an infusion bottle. There are a number of different types of bottles you can get: bottom infused, built in juicers, flip-tops and those with straws built in. Likewise, you can go out on a limb and get a fancy one with all the trimmings that cost a pretty penny or a very basic, inexpensive one. The most important thing is that you do get one and put it to good use.

How an Infused Water Bottle Works

A fruit-infused water bottle has a place to fill with water and a chamber that is separate from the water area for adding fruits, berries and vegetables. The fruit is allowed to mix into the water, adding nutrition and flavor, without imparting the actual fruit into the liquid.

The Big Benefits of Drinking Infused Water

Infused water is a temptation most cannot turn down. It turns ordinary water into a refreshing drink that's loaded with goodness. Here are a few of the benefits of drinking infused water:

- Encourages you to drink more water

- Offers a tasty treat for anyone who is not a fan of water

- Provides a healthy alternative to sodas and sugar-laden drinks

- Offers convenience

- Presents a delicious, economical drink

- Provides even more nutrition than plain water

- Keeps you hydrated

- Promotes weight-loss

There you have it in a nutshell, or in a peel! If you've been skirting the fence, wondering whether to invest in an infusion bottle, it's clear to see that it's a smart choice for a gallon of reasons. Speaking of gallons, not only are there infusion water bottles, but there are pitchers, which are great for parties and to get the family drinking more water.

Chapter 2
Some Fruits Have It and Some Don't

When it comes to infusing, some fruits naturally have what it takes to send their tasty goodness and health-filled nutrients bursting into the water upon contact. Others, like bananas for instance, do not. They will turn brown and are too thick and mushy. Some simply lose their health benefits in the mix. But don't worry, we've done the homework for you. Here's a compiled list of the best of the best fruits for infusion:

1. Tart Cherries

Tart cherries add yummy taste, loads of nutrients and many health benefits to your water. While cherries are one of the smallest fruits, they bring a pint-size package of explosive resources to the table. Be sure to use the tart (sour) variety because the sweet ones are usually best when cooked.

Enjoyed since around 70 B.C., cherries not only fill your glass full of flavor, they will keep your body in tip-top shape as well. They contain anthocyanins (flavonoids) that activate fat-burning molecules. Anthocyanins can boost your brain power, especially the cognitive functions, and lower your blood pressure.

The near-magical mini-fruits are bursting with benefits so potent, they are said to fight inflammation, infections and even cancer due to their high content of quercetin and ellagic, which can stop the spread and growth of tumours. In addition, they are rich in anti-oxidants, melatonin (for sleep), fiber and vitamins C and E. So there you have it. All that…and a cherry on top!

2. Cranberries

Another terrific tiny treat, cranberries provide a powerhouse of goodness. Cranberries are wildly popular in infusions for both taste and health benefits. Many love the slightly bitter twang of the berries, but if you are not a big fan, they can be mixed with other fruits, like cherries, so you can enjoy the nutritional value with only a hint of the flavor. On another note, cranberries have an acquired taste, so if you do blend them with another fruit, you might soon find that you really do like them after all.

Native to North America, the dark-colored berries were used by Native Americans for food and to color rugs long before the Pilgrims set foot on the land. They are rich in phenolic flavonoid phytochemicals, phenolic acids, fiber, manganese, copper and vitamins C, E and K. They are oozing with anti-oxidants that fight off free radicals. Free radicals cause illnesses, diseases, accelerated aging and a host of other problems. Notorious for battling away urinary tract infections, cranberries also help prevent cancer and boost the immune system.

3. Pomegranate

A fruit so beloved it is mentioned in the Bible and featured in ancient art, the pomegranate is loaded with flavor and benefits for your health as well. Infused into your water, this fun and exotic fruit is sure to be a splash.

Pomegranates are a "super fruit," packed with granatin B and punicalagin, which reduce the risk of heart disease and help to clear the body of scavenging free radicals at the same time. They are also bursting with vitamin C, B-complex and vitamin K and contain good amounts of fiber, calcium, copper, and folates.

The dark red fruit explodes into water with nutrients that promote skin health, regenerate cells, and accelerate wound healing; they even have anti-aging qualities. Who knew such a delicious fruit could offer so much?

4. Grapefruit

Now, here's something to sip on if you want to boost your immune, help keep cancer away and lose weight all at the same time. Grapefruit, botanically classified as a berry, was once called the "forbidden fruit." It contains around 60% of the daily dietary recommendation of vitamin C and is also full of vitamin B, fiber, flavonoids, minerals and anti-oxidants (like lycopene), which gives it its nice pinkish coloring.

Grapefruits promote great vision, skin elasticity and healthy mucus membranes. They also help guard against cancer, infections and fungus. In addition, they promote cognitive health. A grapefruit's weight-loss qualities are due in part to its content of the fat-burning substance nootkatone as well as the metabolism-boosting characteristics it holds. Imagine, a fruit that you can add into your infuser that will make you smart and skinny! And just a side note, if you don't care for the bitter burst of flavor in grapefruit, you can add in a splash of lime, lemon and/or orange.

5. Kiwifruit

Did you know that kiwifruit has more vitamin C content than grapefruit? The small, tangy, tropical treasure tips the scale with 85% of your daily recommendation of vitamin C. In addition, it is rich in vitamins K and E, fiber, copper, potassium, phytonutrients and folate.

It has recently been discovered through exhaustive studies that kiwifruit may protect DNA. And it has been proven that they are reaming with anti-oxidants to ward away diseases and other medical conditions. The special mix of phytonutrients and minerals in the fruit help keep stroke, heart conditions, cancers and respiratory diseases at bay. Go green with this tantalizing fruit and you'll get a merry mix of health benefits and a delightful flavor to go along with it.

6. Blueberries

The official fruit of the state of New Jersey, blueberries are one of America's most beloved ingredients for breakfast muffins and for infusions too. Loaded with vitamins A, C, E and B complex, copper, zinc, manganese, potassium, selenium and anthocyanins, blueberries are rich in anti-oxidants that help you fight off diseases.

If you are fortunate enough to hand pick them, you may find they have a light layer of fine dust on them. Don't brush them off; they are healthier and tastier with the dust on.

Blueberries help to keep your blood pressure down. They can improve your memory and boost your energy level too. You'll never be blue with these berries in your glass.

7. Lemons

If you're a lemon lover, you'll be pleased to know that lemons make some of the best infusions ever. Not only are lemons bursting with refreshing flavor, they are overflowing with health benefits too.

In 1493, Christopher Columbus brought lemon seeds with him to America and the nation has been in love with them ever since. You will find vitamins C and B-complex, copper, iron, citric acid, phosphorus, potassium, magnesium, calcium, fiber and flavonoids within the yellow peel of the sour fruit. Lemons help to balance the PH in your body, are awesome for your liver and are rich in anti-oxidants that can keep colds and flus at bay. So don't forget to add a squeeze of lemon in your infused water, straight or mixed with other fruits or berries.

8. Cucumbers

For a delicious drink that is cool as a cucumber, add in some slices of this 3000-year-old fruit. Often mistaken for a vegetable, cucumbers are actually botanically classified as fruits. They are oozing with vitamins like A, K, C, B1, B2, B5 and B6 and are rich in iron, magnesium, calcium, zinc, potassium, folic acid and phosphorus.

Appreciated for their anti-aging abilities, cucumbers are also good for lowering cholesterol, curing bad breath and hydrating the body (they contain 90% water). If you've never infused the crisp, fresh taste of this highly nutritious fruit, it's time to give it a try. They are surprisingly delicious.

9. Peaches

The symbol for longevity in China, peaches make excellent infusions because they are so juicy. Loaded up with vitamins A and C, the fuzzy fruits also have their share of fiber, niacin and potassium.

Peaches are antimicrobials and anti-oxidants as well, so they fight germs of many kinds. They are fabulous for your skin too. If you are looking for a really peachy drink, slurp on this fine fruit.

10. Oranges

Infusing with orange is just what the doctor ordered and tastes refreshing as well. This citrus fruit is named for its color and has a host of nutrients inside the peel like vitamins B, B1, A and C. Folate, pantothenic acid, fiber, calcium, copper and potassium are abundant as well.

Feel like you're coming down with a cold? Slice up some orange and infuse it into water to stave off a cold. Oranges are great for heart health and your skin too.

11. Blackberries

Drink this in: blackberries are so healthy, during the Civil War, soldiers were given orders to pick them in order to keep dysentery away. There is even a name given to the study of blackberries: "batology." Yes, blackberries are *that* important!

Blackberries work wonderfully to infuse into water. They have a sweet taste, too!

12. Raspberries

Each raspberry contains around 100 pieces of tiny fruit. Vitamins C, E and K can be found inside the dark-colored gems in addition to magnesium, folate, omega-3 fatty acids, biotin and potassium.

Raspberries contain a high concentration of a phenolic compound and ellagic acid that helps prevent cancer by actually halting the growth of cancerous cells. If that's not reason enough to add a handful to your bottle, I don't know what is. Did I mention they are sweet, tangy and quite yummy as well?

13. Limes

Loaded with vitamin C, fiber, phytochemicals and anti-oxidants, this sour green citrus fruit is so healthy, one per day was allotted to soldiers in the Civil War to help keep disease and illness away.

Limes are delightful as a single-ingredient infusion and they mix well with a number of other fruits. Add a dash or a big splash, your call!

14. Strawberries

Strawberries delight in being delightfully different and first class, all the way. Generally, the first berry or fruit to pop up for the season, strawberries wear their hearts on their sleeves, or rather...their seeds on their skin.

One of the all-time favorites for infusing, just six to eight strawberries will give you a whopping 160 percent of your recommended daily allowance of vitamin C. In addition, they are jam-packed with folic acid, fiber and anti-oxidants.

Strawberries lend themselves to miraculous health benefits, especially for the blood. They can help lower blood pressure, improve blood flow, replace worn out blood vessels and promote great heart health. Strawberries are juicy and work well in an infusion alone; they mix well with other fruits and berries too.

15. Watermelon

Weighing in heavy in both the nutrition and taste department, watermelons make fun fruits to infuse into your water. Grown in ninety-six countries in the world, watermelons are naturally nutritious and refreshing. Surprisingly, watermelons aren't really fruits. They are vegetables in disguise.

Watermelons are excellent to infuse because they quench your thirst plus they contain a number of key beneficial ingredients for your health like lots of vitamins A and C, lycopene, potassium and so much more. They have the innate ability to reduce inflammation, and since inflammation generally causes pain, you might just say they are a pain reliever. Watermelons are loaded with anti-oxidants so they fight off free radicals trying to destroy your body with cancers and diseases. Fresh off the vine, watermelons make a sensational summer drink that will boost your spirits and your health as well.

As you can see, there are a myriad of fruits and fruit combinations that work well with a water infuser. We'll get into the step-by-step recipes a little later in the book.

Chapter 3
Infused Water vs. Fruit Juice

Which is better, infused water or fruit juice? As flavor goes, it is certainly a matter of taste, literally speaking, but there are some other comparisons to be made as well. Let's take a look.

Nutrients and Calories

Juice is generally fairly nutritious but it's packed with sugar; sometimes natural and sometimes artificial sweeteners are added too. Not only is sugar (natural or not) hard on your blood sugar, it spikes and then drops, leaving you tired and sleepy. Fruit-infused water, however, is low in calories, contains no processed sugar or artificial sweeteners and is extremely good for your blood sugar as well as your body's entire system. Infused water requires a lot less fruit than juice does too.

Flavor

Fruit juice has a very strong taste whereas the taste of water infused with fruit for only 15 minutes has a near-magical tangy, fruity and crisp, fresh flavor. The longer the fruit is allowed to infuse, the better the flavor.

Preparation

If you've ever juiced, you know what a chore it is. It is a timely task of pealing, slicing then squeezing, squeezing and more squeezing. Infused fruit in water is super simple. Just add some fruit in the chamber and pour water into the designated spot and bingo…all done!

Are the health benefits different? Absolutely. So, you will want to weigh what you are looking to get out of your drink.

Appearance

One of the most luring things about fruit-infused water is its attractive appearance. Just looking at the cool clear water and brightly colored fruit wets your appetite.

Juice also can look delicious as well. Both look pretty when used at a party or shower.

Hydration

Both infused water and juice hydrate you. The difference would be in the amount you drink. You would not drink the same amount of juice as you would infused water. Infused water is hydration you can carry with you all day and not have to worry about it affecting your blood sugar or calorie count.

Infused water does the job regular water does, and has some bonuses, depending on what fruit you use. Watermelon and cucumbers are high in water content so you get the extra hydration and some crisp flavor to go along with it.

Chapter 4

The Benefits of Drinking Infused Water

Water holds the key to life. Humans, animals and plants cannot live without it. We suffer when we get too little of it and reap the rewards when we get our fair share. Since infused water is enhanced water, all of the benefits of water can be found in it…and then some.

In order to keep your body healthy, it is recommended that you drink a minimum of eight glasses per day. Doing so will help your skin to stay young and healthy looking and your body to be in tip-top shape. Here's why:

- Our bodies are largely made of water. Babies are about 78% water at birth and a grown man's body contains around 60%.

- Water increases energy and helps to relieve fatigue too.

- Water flushes out impurities and toxins.

- Drinking water is conducive to weight loss.

- Water is great for your skin.

- For an all-natural headache remedy…drink water.

- Water boosts your immune system.

- Proper intake of water helps prevent cramps and strains too.

- Drinking water helps prevent constipation.

All Water Is Not Created Alike

Before going any further, it's imperative to state that all water is not the same by any stretch of the imagination. Some is toxic while other is pure and full of benefits.

Here are some fascinating (and somewhat scary) facts about drinking water:

- "100% pure" does not mean the water you are buying is free of impurities. "Pure" refers to the source the water is derived, so it can mean 100% spring water but…what does the spring's water contain?

- "Natural" is a term that is tossed around that can mean practically anything the manufacturer wants.

- Some bottled water is nothing more than tap water.

- There are great sources of bottled water and purification systems that make your tap water great as well. A little research will reveal the sources.

- The Environmental Protective Agency regulates only 91 of more than 60,000 chemicals used in the United States that can seep into the water systems.

- You can obtain information from consumer reports online that will give you facts. One fact we found revealed that Aquafina uses municipal water for their source.

All that having been said, it is extremely important that you drink water and even more important that you make sure the water you drink is clean. It takes a little effort but it is good to know what is in your water. If you drink bottled water, do your homework on your favorite brand. Home water filtration and purification systems are economical and practical options, but they are not fool-proof solutions. Have the final product of water tested once your system is in place. For all of your infusion drinks, be sure your water is good, clean water.

How to Drink Water

There's an art to drinking water. In fact, there are several suggested ways to drink it that can greatly magnify the benefits.

Some experts advise drinking all eight recommended glasses of water at one sitting, or as close to it as you can. The reason being that it will better hydrate your system and will flush out the toxins more thoroughly. Still, hydrating throughout the day is vital whether you load up at one time or not.

There are many doctors and health specialists who swear by drinking lemon water first thing in the morning. Warm water is said to be best. Lemons are a natural detox and when mixed with the warm water, will get you going…in more ways than one.

Wet Your Whistle

Drinking eight glasses plus of water is easy when it tastes good. Fruit-infused water adds that extra flair to a boring bottle of water. When you enjoy the water, you will drink more of it, and studies show that the more water you drink, the more your body will crave. Your body will actually let you know when you are hydrated, as you will be satisfied.

Drinking infused water is making waves for so many reasons. It's simple to make and the fruit adds anti-oxidants, vitamins, minerals and more to the already awesome effects of water. From the fun, functional and fabulous selection of infusion bottles available, to the eye-candy appeal of the finished product, when you add the fruit and water, infused water makes drinking a pleasure!

Chapter 5
Terrific Tips When Starting with Fruit Infusion

There are tons of healthy living fads. In fact, healthy living *is* a fad. Through the years there's been the high carb diet, the no carb and low-carb diets...the grapefruit diet, cabbage soup diet and the no-diet diet. Rest assured though that water never goes out of style.

Healthy living entails eating adequate amounts of fruits and veggies and getting plenty of water. While juicing serves the purpose, it is a hassle. Not only is the process of making it a pain, cleaning up the food processor and other utensils can be a drag as well. Infusion, on the other hand, is quick, easy and painless to put together. If it is a fad, it's the best one ever!

Here are some innovative ideas that will help you dive in to the joy of fruit and water infusions.

Tip 1: Easy does it

If you are not the world's healthiest person, give yourself a break. You didn't get where you are overnight, so don't expect to get out of your jam instantaneously either. Progress, not perfection, is the best way to approach your new endeavour. Give it time and soon the fruit will begin to satisfy your urges and you will begin to replace bad habits with good ones.

Tip 2: Bold is beautiful

As you know, fruits and vegetables have different flavors and various strengths as well. To tantalize your taste buds, you might start with strong flavors that you love so you are tempted to try them again and again. There will be plenty of time to get used to new flavors or to work on liking ones for which you haven't acquired a taste. Go with those you know and love in the beginning.

Lemons, limes, oranges, strawberries and pineapples are some of the more pronounced fruit flavors used in infusions.

You can add additional elements to the equation with other tastes you are especially fond of too like cinnamon, parsley, mint and lavender. Those flavors can also help when trying new fruit combinations or when working to like your less favorites.

Ginger, cayenne pepper, turmeric, chlorella, spirulina and ginger are nutritious and flavorful additions as well. You will learn that the sky's the limit when it comes to getting creative with infusing.

Tip 3: More fruits, easy on the vegetables

Fruits are the chosen ones when it comes to infusions. While veggies are great for you and are loaded with nutrients, fruits tend to be bigger hits because they filtrate into the water more thoroughly and tastefully. The most popular vegetable used in infusing, the cucumber, turns out not to be a vegetable at all, so…fruit is the pick, no matter how you slice it.

Tip 4: Invest in a good infusion bottle

While you don't have to spend a fortune on an infusion bottle, it's important to get one that is of good quality. You certainly don't want one that leaks, tends to mildew or that absorbs aftertaste. The job of an infuser is to merge your fruit and water, not to flub the process up, so choose wisely.

You will also want to get the type that is right for you. There are those that act as mini-juicers and some that have spouts while others have straws. A number are perfect for the office and other ones are more sports-like bottles.

Be sure the bottle you choose is easy to clean. You don't want too many remote nooks and crannies to have to scrub because that will defeat the purpose of the easy, breezy nature of fruit water infusion and will discourage you from making a bottle of it. Plus, it poses potential health risks if you don't get it cleaned out well enough.

Another thing you can look for is the material that is used to make the bottle. You can find plenty that are BPA-free and some come in glass as well. It's worth shopping around to find the best bottle for your personal likes and needs.

Tip 5: Plan out your recipes a week at a time

Much like planning your meals out, figuring out what fruit water infusions you will have is best done a week at a time. That way, you make sure to have the ingredients you need on hand and never have to miss a day or make a mad dash to the grocery store. It's fun to plan ahead with all the great recipes you'll be introduced to in the following part of this book, and you can come up with some inventions of your own as well.

Chapter 6: Basic Infusion Recipes

Here are some basic recipes to get you started. Since water bottles hold different amounts of water, you can adjust each recipe to the amount that your bottle holds. If you have a large one, you can slightly increase the amount of fruit or if it holds less water, you can decrease the fruit a bit as you add less water. Don't be afraid to customize each recipe to your particular tastes. If you have an infusion pitcher, just double the recipe.

Citrus Mojito Soda

One of the best fruit infusions to start out with is Citrus Mojito Soda. It is not actually a soda, so don't worry. It is a mix of lime juice along with soda water, water and a sprig of peppermint.

Lime has a multitude of nutritional benefits. It is conducive for losing weight and fighting a cold, and it perks your energy level up a notch too. Oh, and did I mention it promotes a great metabolism, helping you burn more calories with less effort?

One sip of this Citrus Mojito Soda and you'll be hooked. But, it's all good. In fact, it's delicious…and quite healthy too.

Ingredients:

- 1 pint of club soda

- ¼ purified water

- 1 lime

- ¼ cup of fresh mint leaves

- 1 large orange

Thinly slice the lime and orange into rings. Place the mint sprigs into the jar bottle and pour the soda on top. Put the lime and orange slices into the infuser chamber and shake gently. Refrigerating for a few hours will add an extra crisp flavor to the mix.

Lemon Water with Mint

When it comes to weight loss, lemon water with mint is the undisputed king of detoxing and keeping the hunger away. Also known as lemon water or lemon detox water, this recipe is tasty with a sour-sweet excitement to the taste buds and very simple to make with only two ingredients. It is rich in electrolytes that play a significant role in speeding up weight loss. It is a perfect drink to make in the morning before leaving the house to fulfil your daily responsibilities.

Ingredients:

- 3 cups of water

- 1 large lemon

- A few springs of mint

Cut the lemon in half and give it a slight squeeze into the water then slice it into thin rings. Place the lemon rings and mint into the fruit compartment then add the water to the designated spot. Chill for several hours and drink cold.

Mango Ginger Water

Boost your metabolism and get rid of pain! This fine drink features mango that is a natural remedy for pain and a metabolic booster. When you add in ginger, you will get a double dose of pain relief. Ginger is conducive to weight loss and helps tummy trouble too. So, the next time you have joint pain, cramps or an upset stomach, reach for this infused miracle in a bottle.

Ingredients:

- 3 cups of water

- 1 large mango

- 1 small to medium ginger root

Peel the mango and cut it into small pieces. Chop the ginger into small pieces as well. Place the water in the designated compartment. Mix the mango and ginger then place them into the fruit chamber. Chill for an hour or two before enjoying.

Strawberry Mint Water

Strawberries are one of the most popular fruits for infusing. They are deliciously refreshing and are bursting with vitamins, minerals and anti-oxidants. Mint is a powerful pain reliever and also contains ample anti-oxidants, so if you want to stay healthy, this is the drink for you.

Ingredients:

- 3 cups of water

- A handful of strawberries (5-6)

- A sprig of peppermint or spearmint

Place the water in the designated compartment. Slice the strawberries and place in the fruit basket. Add the mint in with the water or in the fruit basket. Chill for several hours and enjoy.

Blackberry Lemon Water

Blackberries are full of vitamins, minerals and anti-oxidants. They also contain flavonoids, which give them their dark, gorgeous color. Lemons are loaded with vitamin C and anti-oxidants. Together, these two pack a powerful punch against cold, flus and any other bug that might come your way. They are one of the most delicious combinations on the planet too, so…drink them up.

Ingredients:

- 3 cups of water

- 8 blueberries

- 1 lemon

Fill the water compartment with water. Add the blueberries to the fruit chamber. Slice the lemon and add the slices in with the blueberries. Chill for at least one hour.

After-Work out Infused Water Recipes

After a strenuous workout, your body needs to be replenished. Water is a must and fruits provide nutrients and minerals that are vital post-exercise as well as before. Fruits and water both help boost your energy level and help you to shed body fat while assisting in maintaining and building lean muscles. The combination also helps you to increase your metabolism. These recipes will help you to recover from all that you have put out in your workout.

Watermelon Water with Rosemary

This watermelon and rosemary-infused water drink is the ideal, refreshing tonic to enjoy after a workout. It is satisfying and rewarding. Watermelon contains essential vitamins and minerals and tons of water. It adds a sweet blast to the water while rosemary brings its distinguished flavor and nutrients like calcium, iron and vitamins. Rosemary is a natural pain reliever and is awesome for the circulatory system.

Ingredients:

- 3 cups of water

- 2 slices of watermelon

- 1-2 sprigs of rosemary

Slice the watermelon into small cubes. Then place the rosemary and watermelon into the fruit compartment. Add the water and drop the infuser into the water bottle. Refrigerator for at least 10 minutes before serving or longer if you wish.

Peachy Mint Infused Water

This delicious, nutritious drink gives your tired body what it may be craving: nutrients and hydration. Peppermint is known to be a pain reliever, so your aching muscles will thank you for the addition of it in this peachy drink.

Ingredients:

- Two peppermint sprigs

- 2 medium ripe peaches

- 3 cups of water

- Ice cubes (optional)

Peel and cube or slice peaches and drop them in the fruit basket followed by the mint springs. Fill the water compartment with water and ice. Shake and enjoy. If you don't want to add ice, you can chill the drink for at least 30 minutes instead.

Orange You Needing to Detox?

This drink will help to rid your body of toxins. Coupled with the workout, your body will be on its way to soaring heights with this drink. It's refreshing and will help your body lower its temperature and replenish its water supply, and it's all done deliciously. Plus, it will help get rid of toxins that hold you back from being at your ultimate peak of health. It will cleanse your blood and your digestion.

Ingredients:

- 3 cups of water

- 1 orange

- 1 lemon

- 5 slices of cucumber

- Two fresh mint sprigs

Slice the orange and the lemon into thin rings then load them in the fruit basket. Slice the cucumber into thin pieces and add them in the fruit compartment as well. Place the mint on top and add the water. Shake a little and refrigerate for an hour or longer.

Chapter 6
Infused Water Recipes for Parties and Special Events

The next time you throw a party, why not serve infused water? It's a refreshing beverage that is also very economical and it always makes a splash of presentation.

One disadvantage of sending your kids to a birthday party is that you know they'll be pumped full of sugar. Parents of your little guests will delight in the fact you chose a healthier route.

If you are planning a wedding event, you can color-coordinate the fruit you use. Green weddings are complimented by mint sprigs and limes while strawberries and cherries blend well for black and white or primary-colored ones.

Rustic weddings and events are all the rage right now, so you can easily get by with serving the infusions in Mason jars.

Simply make up a big batch in extra-large bottles or several rounds of smaller ones. Once the fruit has infused into the water, you can pour it into individual serving glasses or into a pitcher and decorate with fresh slices of limes or lemons, a few floating strawberries, sprigs of mint or whatever you choose. You are sure to make a splash when you offer infused goodness to your guests.

Luscious Lemonade Flavored Water

Lemon is bursting with citrus delight. It is refreshing and crisp and oh so healthy! Lemon is nature's best when it comes to reducing fever, curing constipation, warding off colds and flus, dissolving kidney stones and even helping out with dental issues. Vitamins A, C, B6 and E are among the nutrients this delicious drink brings to the table.

Ingredients:

- 3 cups of water

- 1 ripe lemon (or lime)

- 1 ripe orange

- 1 sprig of fresh mint

- Ice cubes (optional)

Slice the lemon and orange and slip into the fruit basket. Give the mints a little squeeze to release the flavor and place in with the fruit. Fill the water and gently shake. Add in the ice or chill for at least an hour.

Berry Lemony Water

For lip-licking goodness and a gorgeous presentation, this mix is impossible to beat. The nutrient content of this pretty combination is out of this world. The berries bring in the vitamins, minerals and anti-oxidants along with rich and bold coloring, and the lemony taste compliments it all with a burst of crisp tang.

Ingredients:

- 3 cups of water

- 1 cup of mixed berries (raspberries, blueberries, blackberries, etc.)

- 1 lemon

Slice the berries and place in the fruit basket. Slice the lemon and add to the berries. Add water and chill at least one hour. To get the maximum benefits from this drink, enjoy immediately.

Tropical Paradise Pineapple and Orange Infused Water

This taste-of-the-tropics drink is like a retreat for your body. It supplies it with anti-oxidants, vitamins and minerals and fat-burning ingredients as well. It's a true tropical powerhouse and is delightfully refreshing too. Children love this one, by the way.

Ingredients:

- 1/4 to ½ cup of pineapple

- 1 orange

- Ice

- 3 cups of water

Slice the orange and cube the pineapple. Mix together and place in the fruit compartment. Fill the water area with half ice and half water. Shake gently and allow to infuse for about 30 minutes before serving.

Blue Hawaii Water

Fantastic for blue color schemes and for tropical or water-themed parties, this drink is loaded with fresh flavor and anti-oxidants too. Blueberries are one of the most popular fruits for infusions and are well-loved by all.

Ingredients:

- 3 cups of water

- 1 hand full of blueberries (about 6-8)

- ¼ cup of pineapple

Cut the pineapple into chunks and slice the blueberries in half. Place in the fruit compartment and add water. Chill for a few hours and then serve.

Kiwi and Lime Water

For a quick pick-me-up for kids or adult guests, this drink offers nutrition and visual appeal. It goes well with many themes and color schemes too, so serve this one with the confidence that it will be a sure hit.

Ingredients:

- 3 cups of water

- 1 kiwi

- 1 lime

- 1 sprig of peppermint or spearmint

Slice the kiwi and lime. Scrunch the mint in your hand and add all three to the fruit basket. Fill the water compartment with water. Chill for at least one hour and serve cold.

Chapter 7
Healing Infused Water Recipes

From migraines to digestive issues, these recipes contain ingredients that may help heal. Fruits like watermelon are excellent for your heart health. Grapefruit assist in keeping your weight maintained, which helps prevent many medical conditions too. The addition of peppermint, and ginger are also full of health benefits. No matter your health complaint, you are sure to find a recipe for you!

Awesome Aloe Water

Aloe vera is known for its healing powers of the skin. It provides cooling and healing relief for a number of conditions like sunburns, indigestion, heartburn and even cancer. The succulent goodness is rejuvenating and refreshing as a drink as well.

Ingredients:

- 2 medium aloe leaves

- 1 lemon

- 3 cups of water

Rinse the aloe leaves and split them lengthwise. Cut them into small pieces and place in the fruit compartment then slice the lemon and add it in as well. Fill the designated area with water. Chill for an hour or two and serve cold.

No Doctor Needed Apple Cinnamon Water

Apples are one of the healthiest fruits. They are bursting with health benefits like fiber, vitamins and minerals. They also contain phytonutrients that ward away heart disease, cancer and other serious illnesses. Cinnamon is a potent spice that brings much to the table like anti-oxidants and is anti-inflammatory, so it helps with swelling and pain.

Ingredients:

- 3 cups of water

- 1 apple

- 1 cinnamon stick (not cinnamon powder)

Slice the apples and discard the core and seeds. Chop the cinnamon stick into small pieces. Mix the apples and cinnamon together and place in the fruit dispenser. Fill the water compartment with water, shake gently and chill for about one hour.

Cure-All Apple Cider Vinegar Water

Apple cider vinegar is known for helping with gorgeous youthful-looking skin. It also helps with digestive issues, heart health and in maintaining balanced blood sugar levels. Apple cider vinegar is high in acetic acid, so it kills bacteria and germs.

Ingredients:

- 3 cups of water

- 1/3 cucumber

- 1 lemon

- 1 sprig of peppermint

- 5 tablespoons of apple cider vinegar

Thinly slice the lemon and cucumber. Mix the two together and place in the fruit dispenser. Give the mint a gentle scrunch and add to the fruit. Place the vinegar into the water compartment and add water. Gently shake and chill for several hours.

Chapter 8
Detoxing Infused Water Recipes

Cleansing your body of toxins is one of the ways you can truly be healthy. We come into contact with so many things that are harmful to our bodies every single day. We drink drinks and eat foods that are laden with harsh chemicals (like pesticides) and GMOs. We breathe polluted air and even use toxic ingredients on our skin, which can be found in lotions, shampoos and even make-up. It's time to detox!

Flush the poison out with these delicious drinks. You will then be able to be healthy and may very well drop a few pounds too. Plus, ridding your system of culprits helps give you energy, and who couldn't stand to have a little more pep?

Trim Down and Slim Down Detox Infused Water

For an easy and effective recipe to cleanse your system of toxins and ditch digestive tract blocks, here is a miraculous, mouth-watering drink that will help you out and will also help to trim up your tummy.

Ingredients:

- 3 cups of water

- 1 grapefruit

- 1 lime (or lemon)

- 1 sprig of mint

Thinly slice the lime and grapefruit. Mix them together to combine the citrus flavors and place them in the fruit compartment. Add the mint after pressing gently on it to release the flavors. Pour in the water. Gently shake and chill for about one hour. Serve cold.

Jazzy Blueberry Orange Detox Water

Who says a detox has to be yucky and boring? This detox is delicious! Blueberries not only help your body get rid of poisons, it gives it metabolic support and promotes your immune system too. Oranges are extremely rich in vitamin C, which will help to keep colds and flu away and will boost your energy level too.

Ingredients:

- 3 cups of water

- 1 cup of blueberries

- 1 ripe orange

Slice the orange into thin slices and cut the blueberries in half. Add to the fruit chamber. Pour the water into the designated area then give a gentle shake. Chill for at least one hour and enjoy cold.

Blueberry Lavender Water

Lavender is calming and relaxing when enjoyed in aromatherapy, but did you realize you can drink it too? Many sleepy-time teas are made from lavender and now, a wonderful detox infusion is as well. Blueberries add a tart, sweet flavor and come with some pretty stout detoxification properties too.

Ingredients:

- 3 cups of water

- 1 cup of blueberries

- 1-2 sprigs of lavender flowers.

Gently take the flowers off of a lavender plant. Cut the blueberries in half. Add the lavender and fruit to the dispenser section of your bottle. Add water and chill for a minimum of one hour. Enjoy cold.

Chapter 9
Super-Powered Fruit and Vegetable Infusion Recipes

Isn't it nice to know that you have access to nature's medicine chest right at the tip of your tongue? These super-powered infusion recipes below are oozing with health benefits and are overflowing with flavor.

You can always adjust the recipes according to your own likes, such as substituting lemon for a lime if that is your preference. You can also customize according to any medicinal needs you have. If your body is aching, add some mint to a recipe even if it doesn't call for any. By now you are becoming a pro, so let's roll on.

Powerful Fruit Basket

This infusion of fruits will have you in ultimate health in no time. It is absolutely loaded with nutrients and is one of the most delicious drinks you will ever have.

Ingredients:

- 3 cups of water

- 5 strawberries

- 3 blueberries

- 3 raspberries or blackberries

- 1 orange

- 1 lime

Slice the orange and lime into thin slices. Poke the berries with a fork to release their juices then combine together and place in the fruit compartment of your bottle. Fill the designated water area with water. Give a gentle shake to join the flavors then allow to chill for one hour.

Minty Lemon Water

When it comes to detoxing impurities out, lemon and mint go hand in hand. They work together synergistically to move poison out of your body while replacing it with anti-oxidants and other nutritional benefits. This is a great beverage to enjoy a few times a week.

Ingredients:

- 3 cups of water

- 1 large ripe lemon

- 2-3 mint sprigs

Slice the lemon thinly and add the mint on top of the slices. Place in the fruit compartment. Fill the designated water area with water and shake gently. Chill for one hour.

Marvellous Mango Ginger Water

Mango can help prevent cancer. It is fabulous for your skin and eyes too. Ginger contains a substance known as gingerol, which leads to wonderful health benefits. It is a potent anti-oxidant and anti-inflammatory. Together, these two jewels work magic.

Ingredients:

- 3 cups of water

- 1 large mango

- 1 small to medium-sized ginger root

Peel and cube the mango. Chop the ginger root into small pieces. Add the water to the water chamber and then place the mango and ginger into the fruit basket. Gently shake and refrigerate for an hour before drinking.

Wonderful Watermelon Water with Rosemary

Although about 92% of a watermelon is comprised of water, the remaining 8% is concentrated goodness like vitamins A, B6 and C. It is bursting with lycopene, amino acids and anti-oxidants not to mention potassium. Rosemary is a fragrant evergreen herb that is loaded with nutrients and fabulous aroma, and it boosts your memory and mood as well.

Ingredients:

- 3 cups of water

- 2 slices of ripe watermelon

- 2-3 sprigs of rosemary

Cut the two slices of watermelon into small cubes. Place them in the infuser. Add the sprigs of rosemary. Pour the water into the water compartment and shake gently. Place the bottle in the refrigerator for 30 minutes or more. Serve chilled.

Cool Peach and Magical Mint Infused Water

Peaches are delightfully delicious. They just pop with flavor. They are loaded with vitamin C and minerals too and peppermint is full of anti-oxidants and the ability to relieve pain. It's a powerful anti-inflammatory as well.

Ingredients:

- 3 cups of water

- 2 medium to large peaches

- 5 mint sprigs

Peel the peaches and cube or slice them and add the mint springs. Place in the fruit basket of your bottle. Add the water and shake gently. Chill for 30 minutes to one hour.

Orangey Luscious Lemon Detox Water

Oranges and lemons are quite a duo when it comes to being healthy ingredients. You'll never catch a cold with this concoction. Great for a summer's day or in the winter when your body is working hard to fight off illnesses that are lurking about, this drink is the ultimate in vitamin C content.

Ingredients:

- 3 cups water

- 1 orange

- 1 lemon or lime

- 1.4 cucumber

- 3-4 sprigs of mint

Chop the orange into thin slices then do the same for the lemon or lime. Slice the cucumber and cut each slice into fourths. Add the mint on top, giving a little squeeze to release the flavors. Place ingredients into the fruit compartment of your bottle. Fill the water chamber with water and chill for at least one hour. Drink cold.

Lovely Lemonade Flavored Water

Get skinny and look young all in one sip! While that may be a little bit of exaggeration, this lemon water really does hold terrific and powerful anti-aging qualities and weight-loss ones as well. Enjoy!

Ingredients:

- 3 cups of water

- 1 lemon (or lime)

- 3 sprigs of mint

- 1 sprig of apple mint

Slice the lemon into thin strips. Add the mints giving them each a good squeeze. Place in the fruit basket. Add water and ice then shake gently.

Tantalizing Lemon Berry Water

Raspberries and blueberries have been coveted for their tantalizing sweet, tangy flavors and their high anti-oxidant properties for centuries. They also add a nice splash of color to the drink.

Ingredients:

- 1 cup of fresh raspberries or blueberries (or a mixture of the two)
- 1 lemon

Poke the berries with a fork to release their juices. Thinly slice the lemon and add to the berries. Place in the fruit basket. Add water and chill for at least one hour. Serve cold.

Taste of the Tropics Pineapple and Orange Infused Water

Pineapples are one of the most flavorful tropical treats around. Loaded with vitamins and minerals, they combine well with oranges and lemons that bring a powerful punch of their own. This drink is best enjoyed sooner rather than later so the pineapples don't brown.

Ingredients:

- 3 cups of water

- 1/4 cup of pineapple

- 1 lemon

- 1 orange

Slice the lemon and orange. Cube the pineapple. Place them into the fruit compartment of your bottle. Fill the water in the designated area and shake gently. Chill for 30 minutes.

Aloe Healing Water

Used for medicinal purposes for centuries, the aloe plant is one of the oldest healing plants on record. It possesses a myriad of healing qualities, so drink up.

Ingredients:

- 3 cups of water

- 2 medium aloe leaves

- 1 large ripe lemon

Extract the aloe leaves by slicing them down the middle lengthwise then chopping them into small cubes or slices. Slice the lemon into thin slices and add both into the fruit compartment. Add in the water and chill for 2 hours to get the full effect. Drink immediately for the best results.

Apple Cinnamon Wonder Water

You know the old saying, "An apple a day keeps the doctor away." Turns out it might be true. Apples are jam-packed with nutrients, anti-oxidants and fiber too. Cinnamon is one of the healthiest spices around, so this drink is loaded with goodness.

Ingredients:

- 3 cups of water

- 1 ripe apple

- 1 stick of cinnamon

Slice the apple, making sure to discard the core and seeds. Chop the cinnamon stick into tiny pieces. Combine the apple and cinnamon and place in the fruit compartment. Fill the bottle with water and refrigerate for an hour or two.

Minty Apple Cider Vinegar Drink

Apple cider vinegar is known for curing a myriad of ailments. When you use it in its unfiltered state with the "mother" in it (the head on it), you reap the rewards even more. It is a heavy-duty detox. Lemon and mint are great to add anti-oxidants to the mix.

Ingredients:

- 1 ripe lemon

- 1 cucumber

- 3-4 springs of mint

- 4-5 tablespoons of apple cider vinegar (best with the "mother" in it)

- 3 cups of water

Slice the lemon and cucumber and place into the fruit chamber. Give the mint a little squeeze and put on top of the fruit. Add the cider into the water compartment and then fill the rest of the compartment with water. Gently shake and refrigerate for at least two hours.

Slim Down Solution Detox Infused Water

Packed with anti-oxidants, vitamins and minerals, grapefruit is known for its ability to burn fat. Lemon is a fabulous detox fruit. The two combined will give your mouth a sensational delight.

Ingredients:

- 3 cups of water

- 1 grapefruit

- 1 lemon (can substitute for lime)

- 1 sprig of peppermint

Slice the lemon and the grapefruit. Add the lime after squeezing it in your hand to release the flavor. Place fruit in fruit chamber and add water to the designated area. Refrigerate for at least one hour.

Bountiful Blueberry Orange Detox Water

Blueberries are one of the most potent fruits when it comes to anti-oxidants. It helps ward off diseases and other illnesses. Oranges are fantastic detox fruits. Coupled together, blueberries and oranges will get the job done to rid your body of waste and toxins.

Ingredients:

- 3 cups of water

- 1 ripe orange

- ¾ cups of blueberries

Slice the orange and the blueberries. Place the fruit in the basket. Fill the bottle with water and place in refrigerator for at least one hour. Enjoy chilled.

Best Blueberry Lavender Water

Lavender is loaded with health benefits. It's a potent detoxification catalyst and will calm your mind as well. You can't beat blueberries for their anti-oxidative qualities.

Ingredients:

- 1 cup of blueberries

- 2 springs of lavender flowers

- 3 cups of water

Gently pick the lavender flowers from the plant and add with the blueberries in the infusion basket. Fill the water into the chamber, gently shake and refrigerate for one hour before enjoying.

The Last Drop

With the valuable information you have learned about the wonders of fruit-infused water, you are well on your way to springing up your health.

You have been schooled on the importance of water, the big benefits of fruit and the near magical way the two work together to boost your health and your spirts too.

The tried and true recipes within this book provide you with a variety of classifications, such as detox and weight loss, after workout drinks and basic ones as well. You can use them verbatim or add your own flair according to your liking. These fruit-infused water recipes are busting with life, and life is delicious. Drink up!

About The Publisher

14 Peaks is a publishing company that was started after the founder finished an extreme race called Primal Quest. After numerous requests for race details, the search for a platform to tell the story began. With the help of the talented CJ Jerabek, the story went to print.

After coaching for 25 years and teaching martial arts for 10, she put together a new kind of team, a publishing team. It takes a great team to help authors showcase their hard work and that is the vision.

"You don't have to be an expert at everything; you just have to bring in those who are."

Wonderful, experts were brought on board that make a strong team. Professionals, who give expertise in their field, making this a winning publishing company.

Free Downloads for You

14 Peaks publishes a variety of books to help people live adventurous colorful lives. 14 Peaks publishes books for relaxation, sports books, books for healthy living, and of course books for celebrating the time with our dogs.

Find free printable coloring pages and short stories at www.14-peaks.com

Printed in Great Britain
by Amazon

19147716R00047